The F Lifeline:

A biblical guide to choosing & maintaining godly friendships

Erica Grant

The Lord rejoices over you
(Zephaniah 3:17). I pray
your friends do as well.

Erica Grant

This book is dedicated to my daughter as well as every woman who took time out of her schedule to tell me about her personal experiences in friendships. I consider it an honor to hear your stories and learn from you. I pray God blesses you with healthy, life-giving friendships. May He give you the boldness to love, forgive, encourage, and uplift them. May He also give you the wisdom and courage to walk away if necessary.

Special thanks to Megan Hopkins, Beverly Barr, Miranda Evans, April Muldrew, Shayla Donaldson, Kelly Greene, Daret Cannonier, and Rochelle Davis for your special efforts in this project. You are priceless.

Two people are better off than one, for they can help each other succeed. If one person falls, the other can reach out and help. But someone who falls alone is in real trouble. Likewise, two people lying close together can keep each other warm. But how can one be warm alone? A person standing alone can be attacked and defeated, but two can stand back-to-back and conquer. Three are even better, for a triple-braided cord is not easily broken. -Ecclesiastes 4:9-12

CONTENTS

PREFACE

Ever since I was a little girl, I've been fascinated with the concept of friendships. I was a military child so every couple of years I would move which also meant every couple of years I had to make new friends. As a result, I found myself drawn to stories that chronicled the life of friends. I often watched shows such as *Any Day Now, Clueless,* and my personal favorite *Golden Girls*. To this day I enjoy watching Rose, Blanche, Dorothy and Sofia get through tough times over cheesecake. They laughed, they cried and got upset with one another. But through it all, they remained together. Their dedication to one another was admirable and I craved it. Unfortunately, that craving led me to ignore clear warning signs about some friendships. Signs that could have saved me a lot of heartaches but taught me valuable lessons about choosing my friends wisely and recognizing my exit cue. As a believer in Christ, those same experiences led me to seek out examples of biblical friendships. Everything that I've learned, I now consider to be a lifeline. It is my hope that the lifelines within this book will assist you in your friendships both now and in the future.

INTRODUCTION

A man of many companions may come to ruin, but there is a friend who sticks closer than a brother. -Proverbs 18:24 ESV

Friendships can be some of the most joyous parts of our lives. Our friends comfort us, encourage us, celebrate us, and help us get through tough times. Having one true friend in a lifetime is like finding a hidden pearl in the ocean. Having several friendships is nothing less than a miracle. I thank God that I've been fortunate enough to come across many pearls in my life. They encourage me, counsel me, correct me, and help me to see things from a godly perspective. They love me despite my flaws, and I treasure them because of it. I also cherish them because I've experienced the downside of friendship: the unmistakable point where all healthy boundaries cease to exist. I've stayed in them out of a false sense of hope and a naive belief that what was in front of me was not real. I've since learned what Dr. Maya Angelou meant when she wisely stated: "when people show you who they are, believe them."

The following pages include my experiences with friendships as well as the experiences of over 100

Christian women and what I've learned from them. After reading this book, you will have knowledge of what a biblical friendship looks like and the necessary tools needed to maintain them. You will also have the ability to recognize the warning signs of an unhealthy friendship and discern whether or not to remain in it. It is my prayer that the words within this book will help foster godly friendships in your life.

Side note: To fully grasp what women experience in friendships, I've interviewed over 100 women who openly and gracefully shared their experiences. Any reference to female friendships is based on this information as well as my personal experiences. The majority of names written within examples have been changed to protect their identity.

All women interviewed were at least 18 years old and of various educational, economic, ethnic, and marital backgrounds. Every woman involved was a professed believer in Christ. A believer is defined as one who has confessed with her mouth that Jesus is Lord and believes in her heart that God raised Him from the dead.

The Friendship Lifeline:

A biblical guide to choosing &
maintaining godly friendships

CHAPTER 1
Friendship: What is it?

No longer do I call you servants, for the servant does not know what his master is doing; but I have called you friends, for all that I have heard from my Father I have made known to you.
-John 15:15 ESV

Navigating the waters of friendships can be difficult because those involved often have different definitions of what they consider to be a friend. While some people give others the title of a friend the moment they meet them, others take time getting to know others before calling them a friend. With the constant use of social media, it's easy to confuse whether or not someone is truly a friend or an associate on a site.

Many of the women I interviewed defined a friend as one whom they have a mutual love, respect, and care. Much like myself, they view a friend as a trustworthy confidante who accepts them for who they are and shares a common interest.

Jesus had many of friends during His lifetime. Interestingly enough, He refrained from calling the 12 disciples His friends until it was almost time for His departure. When His time to be crucified came near,

He began to fervently pour out teachings, instructions, and warnings to the disciples. While doing so, He said, "No longer do I call you servants, for the servant does not know what his master is doing; but I have called you friends, for all that I have heard from my Father I have made known to you" (John 15:15 ESV). The term friend in this verse comes from the Greek word phílos.¹ It defines someone who is dearly loved or prized in a personal, intimate way. It is a trusted confidante, held dear in a close bond of personal affection.

It is from this scripture that I base my description of a friend. Simply put, a friend is someone with whom you share and entrust your life. Posting pics on social media or giving your opinion on a subject matter is one thing but you should reserve what God has personally spoken to you, your life goals, dreams, fears, challenges, and disappointments for those whom you call friends.

Lifeline: *A friend is someone with whom you share and entrust your life*.

So how do you determine whether or not someone is a friend? Consider the following example. Angela and Janet had known each other for several months. They met through a life group at their church. After finding that they had several things in common, they occasionally went out to lunch and enjoyed one another's company. Angela found herself reaching out to Janet if she needed advice. More so than she did to friends she had known most of her life. Janet always listened to Angela's concerns and offered biblical counsel. She didn't always agree with Angela, but she encouraged her in her life goals. Whenever Angela discussed personal mistakes and setbacks, Janet offered love instead of judgment. Angela, in turn, inspired Janet to get out more and enjoy life. When Janet's father suddenly fell ill and died, Angela cleared her schedule and stayed by her side. She even accompanied Janet to his funeral out of town.

Angela and Janet are friends for several reasons. Not only did they share their life goals and disappointments but they treated one another with mutual love and respect despite disagreements. Their relationship displayed the type of sacrifice Jesus spoke of in John 15:13 when He said: "There is no greater love than to lay down one's life for one's friends." This is exactly what Angela did when she cleared her schedule to be by her friend's side during a difficult time in her life. Janet also displayed a willingness to lay aside her life when she stopped to listen to Angela's concerns and offered wise counsel and encouragement, two essential ingredients in friendships.

In fact, many successful friendships in the Bible include wise counsel and encouragement. When Mary, mother of Jesus, entered the home of her cousin Elizabeth, Elizabeth immediately encouraged and blessed Mary. Upon returning to her hometown in Judah, Naomi continuously gave Ruth, her daughter-in-law whose husband was now deceased, wise counsel. That wise counsel enabled her to establish a household, obtain a husband, and eventually give birth to a son named Obed who was a direct ancestor of Jesus.

Jonathan, the son of King Saul, also wisely instructed and encouraged his friend David on more than one occasion when he saw that his father was determined to kill him. His counsel preserved David's life and enabled him to go on to become king of Judah.

The godly give good advice to their friends; the wicked lead them astray. -Proverbs 12:26

In each instance, the wise counsel and encouragement of a friend gave the person strength to continue in God's plan. But the exact opposite can happen when you heed a friend's ill advice. This truth is evident in the story of King David's son Amnon. Amnon fell in love with his half-sister Tamar but convinced himself that he could never have her. His love grew into an intense obsession that eventually made him sick. His friend Jonadab (described in the Bible as a crafty man) saw that his friend was troubled and asked him what was wrong. When Amnon explained that he was in love with Tamar, Jonadab advised Amnon to pretend to be sick and have the king send Tamar in to serve him. Amnon listened to his friend's advice and ended up raping Tamar. When Tamar's brother Absalom found out what happened, he developed a hate for Amnon and two years later had him killed. In this case, following bad advice led to Amnon's death. But in our everyday lives, bad advice can be just as harmful. It can lead to ruined relationships, the loss of business, lawsuits, financial strain, or any form of bondage. Therefore, it's important to choose friends that give wise counsel. The quality of your life will depend on it.

CHAPTER 2

The Qualities of a Good Friend

The righteous should choose his friends carefully, for the way of the wicked leads them astray. -Proverbs 12:26 NKJV

Just as in the case of Angela and Janet, most friendships develop based on a common interest. It is much easier to get to know someone while doing something that you both enjoy rather than sitting down and trying to find common ground. In fact, having a common interest was one of the top qualities women look for when considering friendships. So if a woman finds out that someone she wants to get to know better loves to shop and she loves shopping as well, it would be in the best interest of both women to go shopping to get to know one another. The initial time spent together gives them the opportunity to determine whether or not they want to continue to hang out.

Now let's pause for a minute and take note of the wording in Proverbs 12:26. It reads to "choose" your friends carefully which means that friendship is a choice and you are the one who determines who that will be. If ever you find yourself in a situation where someone tries to force you into a friendship, take a step back and pray. Ask God to show you how to proceed. He may give you the green go light or He may send flaming red stop signs. In either situation, follow the leading of the Holy Spirit with the understanding that following Christ does not require you to be friends with everyone. It demands that you walk in love towards them.

Lifeline: *Following Christ does not require you to be friends with everyone. It demands that you walk in love towards them.*

Take Jesus for example. The Bible explains that Jesus chose 12 men to walk with Him on a daily basis. Remember that these are the same men that He later calls His friends. If you look closely at Luke 6:12-13, you'll see that He chose those 12 out of a crowd of disciples. Surely some of the others standing there desired to be in this group. But the scriptures don't indicate that it was unfair or unloving for Jesus not to include them. Nor does it show that He randomly selected them or chose them based on appearance or popularity. Jesus spent the entire night in prayer before singling them out. Even then we find that only three of those 12 were in His inner circle. They were permitted to go places and experience things that the other nine disciples were not privileged to see. Jesus even instructed them not to tell the others about those experiences. So we see from the example of Jesus that friendship is selective. However, being selective is not an excuse to mistreat or ignore others because you don't like them. Remember you are to walk in love towards everyone. Your selection of friends, however, should be based on certain qualities as well as personal needs. Therefore, the type of personality that draws an individual will vary based on the person.

There are, however, specific qualities that all believers should look for in a friend. So, what are they?

The number one quality that the women interviewed looked for in a friend is loyalty. It's a noble thing to stick with someone during the good times as well as the bad. However, it is difficult to come across true loyalty. The Bible puts it this way: "Many will say they are loyal friends, but who can find one who is truly reliable" (Proverbs 20:6)? If a friend is loyal, it means that you can depend on her to be there when needed. Such was the case with David and Jonathan (1 Samuel 18-20). Jonathan was poised to be the next king of Israel as King Saul's son. However, upon meeting David after his defeat of Goliath, an immediate bond was forged between them. When it became apparent that God has chosen David to be the next king, King Saul became jealous and attempted to kill David on numerous occasions. Instead of covering up his father's hatred or assisting his father with the murder, Jonathan warned David of King Saul's intentions and helped him escape. He did not cease to be friends with David based on his connection with his father nor did he treat him poorly because of it. All the while, Jonathan was aware that the kingship would pass him and go to David. Still, he reaffirmed his loyalty and maintained it until the day he died in battle.

Jonathan offers a great example of what it means to be loyal but let's consider what loyalty does not include. Loyalty does not mean that you keep secrets that will harm others or go along with doing something illegal or immoral simply because she wants you to. It also doesn't mean that you must stop associating with anyone she does not like or be partial or treat them poorly on her behalf. Lastly, it does not mean that you must submit to any form of physical, emotional, or verbal abuse at her hand. Misuse of any kind is not healthy or biblical. If ever you experience abuse, remove yourself from the situation and pray about the relationship. Do not move forward unless you have clear direction from God concerning what to do next. It is never God's will for you to pledge loyalty or continue to be loyal to a friend that tears you down or leads you down the wrong path no matter how long you've known each other. God has called us to love one another, and those types of behaviors do not display love.

Without the power and help of the Holy Spirit, it is impossible to love others the way God has called us to love (See 1 Corinthians 13:4-7). I don't know one person (including myself) who has gotten it right 100% of the time. However, we are advised, "A friend loves at all times, and is born, as is a brother, for adversity" (Proverbs 17:17 AMP). The term "loves" in this verse comes from the Hebrew word 'ahab and translates as to have affection for.[2] The verse is, in essence, saying that friends have an affection or liking for one another. This affection does not change depending on the circumstance. You may upset or aggravate her (and believe me you will get on each other's nerves) but she will still like you despite those aggravations, and the friendship will continue to grow despite hard times. If a person is only fond of you when times are good and you're capable of doings things to her benefit, she is not a friend. Her affections for you are circumstantial. Choose friends that are fond of you in the good times and bad and will be there for you during adversity. However, make sure you are reasonable in your expectations of others. Being a friend during difficult times means to provide encouragement and emotional support. It may also involve financial help or service on your part. It does not, however, mean your friend must abandon her responsibilities to meet your needs. If she has obligations, such as a family or job, it is unreasonable to expect her to disregard those commitments. Love is a two-way street that involves each of you considering what is best for the other person.

In considering whether or not to become friends with someone you should also take note of the person's temperament and trustworthiness. Proverbs 22:24-25 reads "Don't befriend angry people or associate with hot-tempered people, or you will learn to be like them and endanger your soul." Proverbs 11:13 warns us "A gossip goes around telling secrets, but those who are trustworthy can keep a confidence." No matter what type personality you have, seek out friends that are not easily angered and are trustworthy. The last thing you need is to have someone in your inner circle who gets upset and exposes all of your personal business.

So in considering new friendships or evaluating current ones, ask yourself the following questions:

- Does she give wise counsel?
- Is she encouraging?
- Do I enjoy her company?
- Does she currently have at least one long-term friendship?
- Do we have a mutual respect, fondness, or liking for one another?

- Does she love others?
- Does she help others during times of need?
- Is she slow to anger?
- Is she trustworthy?
- Does she keep information confidential?

If you've answered no to any of these questions, you should reconsider if this person is a friend as previously defined. Maybe you occasionally hang out with her, and you should always remain hospitable, but the person is not likely someone with whom you should share and entrust your life. In the same respect, as a follower of Christ, you should seek to display these same qualities of friendship towards others. If you lack any of these qualities, pray and ask God to help you in that area. Likewise, you should pray and ask God for wisdom and discernment in choosing your friendships. God will freely and willingly grant you wisdom if you ask Him (James 1:5).

CHAPTER 3
The Purpose of Friendship

Two people are better off than one, for they can help each other succeed. -Ecclesiastes 4:9

I love seeing a gathering of two or more women sitting and enjoying one another's company. Whether they are eating a meal, sipping coffee, or getting a pedicure, it makes my heart glad to see them. These get-togethers often include smiles and laughter. Unfortunately, if you watch any popular reality television show involving a group of women, you'd see the exact opposite. The shows usually portray a group of women who dread being in one another's presence. Add in finely manufactured events by the producers, and you've got situations that inevitably breed drama, backstabbing, and gossip.

However, the Bible portrays good friendships in an entirely different way. Healthy friendships are those that enrich both parties' lives and involve helping one another out during difficult times. This is the true purpose of friendship. In Ecclesiastes 4:9-12, Solomon explains it this way: "Two people are better off than one, for they can help each other succeed. If one person falls, the other can reach out and help. But someone who falls alone is in real trouble. Likewise, two people lying close together can keep each other warm. But how can one be warm alone? A person standing alone can be attacked and defeated, but two can stand back-to-back and conquer. Three are even better, for a triple-braided cord is not easily broken."

Lifeline: Healthy friendships are those that enrich both parties' lives and involve helping one another out during difficult times.

Oh, how I would love to sit down with you and listen to your stories of how your friends have helped you in tight situations. Friends have the ability to see our blind spots and warn us just in time. They can tell you about that not so great guy you're dating whom you think is perfectly fine. They can pick you up when you've fallen into painful situations – both those that you've put yourself into and those that life unexpectedly hand delivers. They have a keen ability to see things in a way you can't because you're too emotionally invested or tired. More importantly, they can remind you of who you are in Christ and what He has put you here on earth to accomplish.

A few years ago, I found myself in a painful situation that tested my character and identity in Christ. There was nothing particularly unordinary going on during this time in my life. I was carrying on business as usual when the situation presented itself.

Suddenly, I found myself doubting who I was and whether or not I belonged to Christ. I struggled daily battling negative thoughts concerning it. When I confided in a few close friends about the situation, they enabled me to see it as an attack from the Enemy and reminded me of who I was before I began to accept his lies. This is what the scripture in Ecclesiastes means when it states that one person standing alone can be attacked and defeated, but two can stand back-to-back and conquer. I hate to think of the trouble that would have come my way if I didn't have friends there to help me.

Don't believe the lie that you don't need anyone else in your life and that you can make it on your own. Develop friendships that can help you succeed and encourage you. Disregard the drama-laden, superficial images of friendship created by Hollywood, pop culture, and social media that contradict the scriptures. Despite what those and other banners of pop culture would have you believe, healthy friendships never involve tearing one another down, seeking another's demise, or being deceitful.

CHAPTER 4
The Power of Friendship

Anxiety in a man's heart weighs him down, but a good word makes him glad. -Proverbs 12:25 ESV

It's a beautiful thing to be able to walk through life and enjoy the company of a good friend. Whether you've got one, a few or a dozen, her presence in your life brings about many positive health benefits. In fact, a study conducted by professors at UCLA found that positive female friendships can reduce the negative side effects of stress.[3] In it, the professors explain that women engage in what's called "tending and befriending," a term used to identify the tendency of women to care for their children or flock to their friends during stressful events. After doing so, a chemical called oxytocin (also known as "the bonding hormone") is released and produces a calming effect that reduces fear and the negative side effects of stress. Likewise, a University of Michigan study found very similar results.[4] Women in this study, who had close emotional ties to other women, were found to produce higher levels of progesterone which in turn boosted their mood and alleviated stress.

There's something about meeting with your

friends and talking about your situation that helps ease your burden. Think about the number of times you have walked away from a girl's night out or lunch date feeling relieved. She may not have a solution to your problem, but she'll more than likely empathize with your plight. When it's good news, she'll rejoice with you. If it's bad news, chances are she'll be just as disappointed as you. Hopefully afterward, she'll offer words of encouragement, prayer, and counsel based on God's word. This is what the author of Hebrews intended when he instructed the Church to "not neglect meeting together" (Hebrews 10:25). In fact, not getting together and developing close female friendships can be detrimental to your health. According to the ongoing Harvard Medical School Nurses' Health Study, the lack of a female confidante is just as harmful to a woman's health as smoking or being overweight.[5] Other studies have found that women in low-quality relationships are more likely to have conditions such as heart problems, atherosclerosis, high blood pressure, delayed cancer recovery, and an impaired immune system.[6] Stressful friendships can also contribute to poor health habits such as overeating, heavy drinking, drug use, and smoking as a mechanism to cope with the stress. However, positive female friendships foster a sense of purpose and belonging. They have been shown to reduce blood pressure, heart rate, and the release of stress hormones. In considering these health factors, it is crucial that you choose your friends wisely as they have the ability to either enhance your health or sorely degrade it.

Lifeline: Choose your friends wisely as they have the ability to enhance your health or sorely degrade it.

CHAPTER 5

Types of Friendships

There are 'friends' who destroy each other, but a real friend
sticks closer than a brother. -Proverbs 18:24

I have several different types of friends, and all of
them are valuable. Each one brings a different asset
to my life and can assist in ways that another cannot.
If ever I have a question about what I should wear to
an event, a particular friend immediately comes to
mind. When in doubt, I shoot her a photo text of what
I'm considering and ask for her advice. On the other
hand, if I'm in the middle of a parenting nightmare
(i.e. a power struggle with my strong-willed daughter),
another friend immediately comes to my mind. But,
if I think I'm overreacting about something and need
to hear the God's honest truth of the matter, I call
someone entirely different. Each one of them brings a
valuable element to my life, and I love them for it.

Often problems in female relationships begin
when we mislabel someone as a friend when in
actuality they are destroying us. To determine how
frequently women do this, I adapted a list of several
different types of friends based on *The Friends We Keep*
by Sarah Z. Davis and *Toxic Friends* by Susan Shapiro

Barash.[7,8] When I sat down to talk with different women concerning their friendships, I presented this list and asked them to indicate whether they currently have friends or have had friends in the past that fit the description. I explained that a person would be classified as a particular type of friend if the majority of the description fit her. While one woman could fit into one category, another could fit into three. A total of eight categories were presented and are as follows. While reading the descriptions, keep in mind that many of the negative characteristics associated with a particular type of friend often dissolve as she grows closer in her relationship with God. A more mature believer would look slightly different from the descriptions below. I will reveal a more accurate depiction of a mature believer afterward. The types of friends presented were as follows:

Leader: The leader is the friend that organizes activities and sets the tone for the group. She is often admired by others and determines what's acceptable and what's not. She also determines who's in a group of friends and who's not. She can sometimes be more concerned about her status than the well-being of others in the group and is prone to thinking that she is in charge of other people's lives.

Doormat: The doormat is the friend who takes on the problems of others. She is cautious, moral, shy, and likes to please others. She can also be loyal to a fault and indulges others in their problems thinking of herself as a savior. She is not critical but can be a martyr. Oftentimes she doesn't share her own problems.

Misery Lover: This person is a friend out of convenience. The relationship is birthed out of an unfortunate circumstance such as the death of a loved one, loss of a job, a divorce, or any other type of personal setback. It only thrives if both parties involved are experiencing sadness. She will open up and offer secrets as a gateway to finding out yours. However, once your situation begins to turn around, she will pull away. The focus of the relationship is about your bad news rather than good.

User: This person is overly interested in you from the beginning. She will quickly attach herself to you and your crowd. She is usually very charismatic and enticing. She can also be nosy and intrusive. Her actions are purposeful, deliberate, and self-serving. Your well-being is not of concern to her.

Frenemy: This person appears to be a close friend but later reveals negative feelings or signs of betrayal. She has a designated plan in mind from the beginning and is manipulative. She is untrustworthy, deceitful, and narcissistic. If the opportunity presents itself, the relationship becomes invisible. It is possible that she idolizes and despises you at the same time.

Trophy Friend: This friend is well connected in her community. She is usually charismatic, passionate, and intimate but lacks commitment. She is winsome because of her grace, popularity, and intelligence. However, she usually seeks out others to elevate herself to a new level. Streaks of meanness usually show up after the relationship has developed.

Sharer: This friend is positive, genuine, trustworthy, and dependable. She is always there during emergencies and is in it for the long haul. She is also a good confidante. She gives and shares everything she has with expectations for you to do the same. She expects some form of appreciation and can be emotionally tolling as others may not be able to give the same amount of effort as she does. She pours herself into the relationship because she desires to be your best friend and yearns for closeness.

Authentic Friend: This individual is deeply committed to the relationship. She is tolerant of her friend's entanglements and can see her friend more clearly than the friend can see herself. She is forgiving, accepting, and sincere. She does not seek out what's in it for herself but operates on mutual self-esteem, care & flexibility. She will reinvent her role and adapt with time. She is uninterested in competition and enhances your life as well as gets you through tough times.

Of all the descriptions listed above, only five would qualify as a friend. Remember a friend is someone with whom you can share and entrust your life. Users, frenemies, and misery lovers are not real friends. You should not share and entrust your life to them. In fact, frenemies and users are those whom the scripture above refers to as "friends who destroy each other." Stay away from those types of "friends." They would have to do some serious growing and make a complete 180 degree turn around to be considered a real friend. However, there is a bit more hope for the misery lover if they come out of their state of misery and learn to celebrate the victories of others.

Lifeline: Users, frenemies, and misery lovers are not real friends. You should not share and entrust your life to them.

Now let's consider the real question many of you were probably wondering when reading the descriptions of the user, frenemy, and misery lover. If you're anything like me, you were probably wondering if these women were followers of Christ. The answer is a resounding yes. 63% of friends classified as misery lovers identify as believers (one who has professed with her mouth that Jesus is Lord and believes in her heart that God raised Him from the dead). Likewise, 55% of users and 58% of frenemies identify as believers. In reality, whether or not she had accepted Christ was not the issue. Her maturity and growth in Christ, however, was. Individuals who are more mature in their faith do not exhibit these types of behaviors. Nevertheless, even mature believers fall short of God's standards.

Those that fit the description of a leader, doormat, trophy friend, sharer or authentic are friends. But the first four require a little patience and effort on the part of those who are closest to them.

A leader, for example, would require patience if she has not matured to a point where she understands that she is not in charge of other people's lives. As she matures, she will respect other people's decisions even if it's contrary to what she feels is best for them. She will also consider the needs of others instead of only looking out for herself.

Doormats would require a lot of effort to establish trust and get to a point where they feel comfortable enough to share their problems. As they mature, they will share what's going on in their personal lives and shed their savior complex.

The trophy friend, on the other hand, would require both effort and patience since trust is difficult to establish with those who continuously break commitments and do mean-spirited things. A mature trophy friend will keep her word and be graceful in her speech and actions towards others.

Sharers would also require patience as they learn to accept that everyone gives and shows appreciation in different ways. A mature sharer welcomes any form of recognition and understands that not everyone can give as she does nor are they required to do so.

That leaves us with one last type of friend: the authentic. Coming across an authentic friend is rare. Just like anyone else, she has imperfections that will vary by person. However, if you've got one of these, then God has undoubtedly blessed you. Hold on to her for dear life. She is the embodiment of a friend who sticks closer than a brother.

CHAPTER 6

The Challenges of Friendship

Faithful are the wounds of a friend; profuse are the kisses of an enemy. -Proverbs 27:6 ESV

Every friendship has challenges. Whenever you have two different personalities getting together, there is potential for conflict or disagreement. How you handle the disagreement or conflict will determine the future of the friendship. If you are accepting of the other person's differences and if you are apologetic when you've committed a wrong, the relationship will fare well. But if you hold tightly to the notion that the person must think, believe, or act in agreement with your preferences or if you refuse to acknowledge any of your wrongdoing, then you're in for a bumpy ride.

Take Carla, for example. Carla was very generous in offering her opinion concerning the life of her friend Laney. She fully expected Laney to accept her views just as easily as she freely gave them. But when the tables turned, and Laney attempted to offer advice concerning Carla's personal life, Carla would not allow it. This created distance in the friendship, which in turn strained the relationship.

Gabby, on the other hand, was having car

troubles. As her friend, McKenzie, drove her home, she began to make phone calls to find a way to work the next day. After exhausting all possibilities to no avail, she turned and asked McKenzie for a ride the next day. McKenzie responded by requesting that Gabby use her as a backup option which upset Gabby. Some time later Gabby expressed how she felt, and McKenzie apologized. Thankfully, they are still friends today. Gabby's courage to be honest with McKenzie prevented the friendship from deteriorating and reflects one of the top traits women look for in female friends. When asked why one considered her best friend to be her best friend, I received the following top 5 traits (in order of significance):

1. Loyalty
2. Encouragement & support
3. Honesty
4. Non-judgmental & accepting of who they are
5. Ability to remain close despite not talking daily

The friendships that lasted beyond decades included respecting one another's decisions, allowing one another to have a difference of opinion, telling one another the truth without overstepping boundaries, and apologizing after committing a wrong. On the other hand, relationships that involved drama, co-dependency, lying, jealousy, negative competition, and a lack of confidentiality often dissolved. When asked about the most common issues experienced in female friendships, the top 5 challenges were reported (in order of significance):

1. Jealousy
2. Lack of time spent together
3. Miscommunication
4. Competition
5. Lack of trust

Such challenges in friendships can either make the relationship stronger or cause a rift. When dealing with the following issues be sure to step lightly.

CHAPTER 7

The Green-Eyed Monster

Anger is cruel, and wrath is like a flood, but jealousy is even more dangerous. -Proverbs 27:4

Jealousy is a commonly used but widely misunderstood word. Oftentimes it's casually thrown around in statements like "I'm jealous that you're going on vacation" or "I'm jealous of your beautiful hair." Sometimes we even classify others as being jealous when in actuality they admire a quality, lifestyle, or position that someone embodies. But jealousy is far more than that. Jealousy says I want what you have, but I also don't want you to have it. Jealousy says I deserve that promotion, position, man, status, ministry or any other thing you've set your eye on more than the other person. Jealousy says to do what is necessary to take it away or at the very least diminish the individual who has it. It is nowhere near a harmless feeling of desiring what someone else has and always works in the opposite way a person intends. In fact, the Bible indicates that jealousy is a spirit that seeks to do harm towards others (James 3:15).

Take the case of Daniel. Daniel performed his job

duties in Babylon with such excellence that the king desired to put him over all the other governmental officials (Daniel 6). When his co-workers found out, they became jealous and sought to find fault in him. After finding no ground for complaint, they decided to devise a plan against him in connection with God's commands. They went directly to the king and advised him to create an irrevocable law that prevented anyone in the land from praying to anyone except him over the next 30 days. Anyone who did pray to another god would be thrown into the lion's den. The king, oblivious to their plan, agreed and signed the law. Meanwhile, Daniel who was aware of what had just taken place went home and prayed as he always did in open view. The officials caught him in the act then hastily went to tell the king what they had witnessed. However, the king's response was not what they expected. Instead of immediately ordering Daniel to be placed in the lion's den, the king was greatly distressed and sought to find a way out of it. Hours later the officials remind him that the law cannot be reversed and Daniel is thrown into the den. Full of distress, the king refuses to eat and isn't able to sleep. The next morning he rushes to the lion's den and cries out in anguish to Daniel. To his surprise, Daniel is still alive and explains that an angel of God had shut the lions' mouths. The king then orders that Daniel is taken out of the den. But he also orders for the men who devised the plan to be thrown in along with their wives and children. It was an extremely high cost that I'm sure none of them ever expected to pay. But we can all learn a lesson from it: Jealousy never works out the way a person intends for it to. No matter how well planned or full-proof it may seem, it will always backfire on the possessor.

Perhaps you've never had a co-worker conspire against you or devise a plan to take your life so let's look at it from another angle. During college one weekend, Tonya's mother paid her a visit. When she arrived at the dorm room, she presented several dresses and shoes to her daughter and enthusiastically encouraged her to try them on. As Tonya began to try on the dresses, she noticed her roommate making faces and later making comments about how much her mother spoiled her. She went on to say that one of the outfits was ugly. Then later took that same brand new outfit (including the shoes) and wore it without asking. Why? Because jealousy always seeks to take what rightfully belongs to someone else.

Ava, on the other hand, had a close friend with a newborn baby. As a new mother, she allowed others to look at the baby but did not allow anyone to hold him. Sometime later Ava had her first child and gladly allowed others to embrace her baby. As time passed, the friend approached Ava and explained that she loves but hates her because others seemed to favor Ava's baby more than hers. Our lesson here: jealousy always seeks to diminish others.

Can a friendship exist after the presence of jealousy?

While jealousy is often difficult to navigate, it is possible to salvage the friendship if the person is open, honest, and repentant. Of all the women interviewed, 88% of them reported experiencing jealousy either on her behalf or the behalf of her female friend. 24% of those same participants indicated that they now have a great relationship with those same women. If you find yourself becoming jealous of others, confess it as sin and ask for God's forgiveness. Know that God created you with your exact image, personality, talents, and gifts on purpose. He is not holding out on you nor is He confined to blessing one person at a time. Consider that if God has not given you something you desire, then it may not be what's best for you at the moment. In some cases, you may not have what you want because you didn't ask God for it. But in other instances, you do not have what you desire because you ask with wrong motives (James 4:2-3). If what you desire is not within His plans for you, remember that He knows what is best and His plans are always for your good (Jeremiah 29:11). Besides, you never know what someone had to go through in order to get what you desire and you may not be willing to pay the price for it. So celebrate your friend's accomplishments and expectantly wait for God to bless you too.

Lifeline: While jealousy is often difficult to navigate, it is possible to salvage the friendship if the person is open, honest, and repentant.

If you have a friend that you feel is jealous towards you, seek God as to how to proceed. Specifically ask Him whether it is a spirit of jealousy or a misunderstanding on your part. While your feelings are indicators of what's going on in your heart, they are not to be confused with discernment. True discernment is carefully examining the message and actions of others (1 Thessalonians 5:21-22). If you are basing your assessment on feelings alone, you are in error. Remember the spirit of jealousy always seeks to do harm to the person it is directed towards. Ask yourself if she has tried to hurt you or merely replicate something in your life that she admires. If you find that she does embody the spirit of jealousy, go to her privately and discuss the matter. Her reaction will tell you everything you need to know. Watch for the following cues:

- Does she acknowledge or deny the wrongdoing?
- Does she apologize or make excuses?
- Does she accept responsibility or blame you?
- Does she profess to make changes or see nothing wrong with her behavior?
- Does she speak from a place of love or hatred?

Soak in the responses and listen to the voice of the Holy Spirit as to what to do next. Ask yourself, what is God leading me to do in this situation?

CHAPTER 8
Lack of Time Spent Together

Dear brothers and sisters, after we were separated from you for a little while (though our heart never left you), we tried very hard to come back because of our intense longing to see you again. -1 Thessalonians 2:17

As I sit to write this chapter, some close friends of mine and I have attempted to arrange a girl's night out at least four times within the past week. We typically try to get together once a month but with summer schedules, vacations, and a newborn baby, three months have managed to slip right past us. I fully understand Paul's longing to see his friends in Thessaloniki, and with the lack of time spent together being the second most reported challenge in friendship, I'm sure you do too. Take a close look at 1 Thessalonians 2:18. In it, Paul states "We wanted very much to come to you, and I, Paul, tried again and again, but Satan prevented us." Soak in that last part. What was Paul's problem? Was it scheduling or life obligations? No, Paul indicated that the problem was Satan. Now before you begin thinking that it's not that serious, consider the passage in Ephesians 6:12: "For we are not fighting against flesh-and-blood enemies, but against evil rulers and authorities of the unseen world, against mighty powers in this dark world, and against evil spirits in the heavenly places." Let's face it. There are other forces in this world beyond what we see with our physical eyes, and some of them are pure evil. But what does that have to do with you and your friends? Consider that if you've got a group of friends that love, encourage, and hold one another accountable, it is possible that Satan is hindering you from coming together.

The whole purpose of fellowshipping is to build one another up. The purpose of friendship is to help one another succeed. If Satan's purpose is to steal, kill, and destroy, then why would he want you to spend time with someone who prevents him from doing just that. Don't allow him to hinder you from connecting with your girlfriends. It doesn't have to be a night or weekend out (although those are nice). It could be a house visit or a phone call or text simply to say "I'm thinking of you" or "how was your day?" Friendships, like marriage, require work. The more you feed it, the more it grows. If you starve it, it will eventually die. If you feed it occasionally, it will grow occasionally.

**Lifeline: Friendships, like marriage, require
work. The more you feed it, the more it grows.**

Several months ago I received a plant as a gift. While I considered the gift to be an honor, I was equally horrified at the prospect of trying to take care of it. You see, I have a history of starving plants to death. Nothing is safe, not even a cactus. Despite the odds, the plant remains alive. This is largely due to the fact that I purposely placed it next to the kitchen sink so I can remember to water it. Sadly, it is still in the original container (gift wrap and all). Then one day I noticed that the plant is the exact size as it was when I first received it. After doing some research, I discovered that leaving it in a small container and randomly watering it when I feel like it, stubs its growth.

Friendships are very similar. Random feedings will prevent its growth. Unfortunately, a perception exists among women that healthy friendships can go extended periods of time without any interaction and still thrive. While the relationship may continue to exist, it is not growing. Oddly enough, women do not hold any other relationship to the same standard.

For example, would you expect to grow closer in your relationship to God if you rarely spent time with Him in prayer, worship, studying the Bible, or in your everyday life? In a romantic relationship, would you expect to have intimacy if you occasionally spent time with your significant other? In your family life, would you anticipate having close-knit relationships without spending any quality time with them?

The concept of thriving with minimal interaction does not even exist in the workplace. Disaster would ensue if you rarely communicated with your boss, co-workers, or subordinates, especially when working on a group project. Still, in each instance, the relationship continues to exist. In fact, there may be a genuine love, respect, and admiration, between those involved. However, the intimacy, growth, and success within it becomes limited or nonexistent if the individuals do not spend time together.

Sadly, with all the demands of life, it can become easy to place friendships at the bottom of the priority list. There are 24 hours in a day and it is impossible to fit every single person into your schedule. However, if you value your friendships and they add value to you, you must be intentional about planning time with your friends. Don't be overly concerned about the amount of time you have to give. If all you can spare is an hour a week, then give her your undivided attention during that one hour. If all you can spare is one dinner a month, then enjoy your dinner together. If a quick call on your commute home is the most feasible for you, then use that commute time to catch up. The goal is to maintain contact so that the relationship will continue to grow. That connection, no matter how small it may seem, does far more than nothing. So, I'll leave you with this bit of encouragement: "Let us think of ways to motivate one another to acts of love and good works. And let us not neglect our meeting together, as some people do, but encourage one another, especially now that the day of his return is drawing near" (Hebrews 10:24-25).

CHAPTER 9
Miscommunications & Confrontations

If your brother sins against you, go and tell him his fault, between you and him alone. If he listens to you, you have gained your brother. -Matthew 18:15 ESV

One would think that with all the means of communication today, it would be easy to get the point across. However, miscommunication continues to be a common problem. A small comment sent via text or email can lead to hurt feelings or get the ball rolling on World War 3. Often, technology can make it worse leading the reader to interpret the message in a way that the sender never intended. When you send messages via text, email, or private chats, the person on the receiving end is left to assume the tone of the message. The sender may intend to make a friendly gesture or harmless comment, but the recipient may perceive that same harmless comment as an insult. For example, if I type and send a message that reads "Are you going to eat that?" it could be taken several different ways. Consider how you just read it. If you have small children like me, maybe you read it in the tone of a child asking if you're going to eat that with a mental picture of a little hand reaching towards your plate. If you have feelings of guilt concerning what you eat, then you probably read it in a judgmental you know you shouldn't be eating that tone. The list could go on and on.

When communicating things of a sensitive nature, it is always best to talk in person or by phone if that's not possible. It is easier to hurl insults or say mean-spirited things when you are behind a computer screen or other device. I call it the big, bad, bold syndrome. Symptoms include being timid in person but brazenly bold and rude when behind a device. To avoid the syndrome, let your emotions calm down then pick up the phone or meet face to face to speak with the friend with whom you're having a problem.

How should I address it?

A popular strategy used by some in confronting issues is writing letters. People typically use this approach if they shy away from confrontation or have difficulties expressing what they think or feel during one. The apostle Paul wrote many letters to the churches confronting sin (others even accused him of having the big, bad, bold syndrome see 2 Corinthians 10:10). However, he wrote those letters during a time where cell phones, video chatting, and satellite churches did not exist. He had no other means of communicating with his churches if he was out of town. While I understand a person's reasoning behind writing such letters, I do not recommend it. As a recipient of such messages, I'll tell you why. As previously mentioned above, the person receiving the message has to assume your tone concerning the problem. If it's her first time hearing of the issue, she also has to try and remember the incident then guess your frame of mind. This opens a wide gate of assumption and confusion, and God is never the author of confusion. Unless expressly written, she will be left wondering what you are expecting. Is she supposed to write back or meet with you? Hopefully the person sending the letter does not expect to have the final say on the matter. Therefore, the recipient is now in the awkward position of confronting the issue. Yet, the whole purpose of the letter was to try and avoid confrontation.

A better solution would be to use the written letter as a mechanism to get to the root of the problem. Writing, like music or art, is a good outlet to express your thoughts and feelings. It can also be very therapeutic. However, when writing about an issue that bothers you, it is usually raw. It would be foolish to send out messages to others in a state of raw emotion. If you unleash your frustrations or anger out on others, there will be a price to pay. It is usually a breach in the relationship. This is why Solomon declared "Fools vent their anger, but the wise quietly hold it back" (Proverbs 29:11). His father David even stated "Don't sin by letting anger control you. Think about it overnight and remain silent" (Psalm 4:4). Instead of sending the letter, use it to jot down your thoughts. Pray, let your feelings subside, then go back and determine what you need to share with the other person and how to go about sharing it. If you plan on speaking to her over the phone, have your notes in front of you when you address the issue. If you're meeting in person, simply jot down key points you want to discuss, so you remember them after you have begun talking. Otherwise, burn it!

Are confrontations biblical?

Confrontations are never joyful, but they are not a bad thing. We erroneously think that to be loving or forgiving we must sweep any issue we have with others under the rug. Any woman who brings up an issue with another is deemed emotional or overly sensitive. The other individual may even tell her how she should feel about the situation. I have been guilty as charged of these offenses. But, who am I to tell other people how they should feel about a situation (good or bad)? It's faulty reasoning. Jesus himself said: "If your brother sins against you, go and tell him his fault, between you and him alone. If he listens to you, you have gained your brother" (Matthew 18:15 ESV). The point Jesus is making here is to do what is necessary on your part to settle the issue. If something is bothering you, then you should bring it up. However, you should note that Jesus said: "if your brother sins against you." This means that what you are confronting is actually a sin committed against you. If your friend doesn't like your outfit, that's not a sin. She's entitled to her opinion. But if that same friend who doesn't like your outfit makes it a point to insult and belittle you because of it, that's a sin. It goes against the commandment of love. You need to address it.

Even when our friends don't verbally express that something is wrong yet we sense that something is, we are commanded to address it. Matthew 5:23 (ESV) reads "So if you are offering your gift at the altar and there remember that your brother has something against you, leave your gift there before the altar and go. First be reconciled to your brother, and then come and offer your gift." This is another tall order given by Jesus. The word reconciled in this text comes from the Greek word diallassó which means to change or exchange needless hostility.[9] The Miriam-Webster dictionary defines it as to cause people or groups to become friendly again after an argument or disagreement.[10] To be reconciled in essence means to be at peace and on friendly terms with others. In today's world, it would be equivalent to saying, "If you are in a church service offering worship, praise, or monetary donations, and you remember that your sister has a problem with you, stop what you're doing. Go and make things right with her then come back and offer your gift." Our primary goal in talking out miscommunications or confronting issues with friends should always be peace.

Lifeline: Our primary goal in talking out miscommunications or confronting issues with friends should always be peace.

Watch out for the following faulty thinking and peace snatchers during confrontations with friends:

"I'm going to set her straight."

This statement could have easily been my personal mantra in the past. My first instinct in dealing with any issue with a friend was to tell her about herself and get her back on what I felt was the right track. However, in dealing with any problem with a friend, it is never our responsibility to set her straight. Our responsibility is to communicate the offense and remain at peace with her. Only God has the power to change people. We can only suggest changes and pray for them.

"This conversation will end all interactions and communications from this point forward."

I once foolishly thought this. However, even if you will no longer be close friends, you are still required to walk in love towards them when you see them. It doesn't mean that you must get into an in-depth conversation about what's going on in your life. It doesn't even mean that you will feel like embracing her whenever you cross paths. However, your hopes and intentions towards her should be for her best.

"I didn't mean to offend her so she shouldn't be offended."

Whether or not we intend to offend others is entirely irrelevant if she's offended. Even if you feel she is overly sensitive, it is her responsibility to bring any issue she has that involves sin to the table. It is your duty to do your part to settle it even if it means agreeing to disagree.

"She should know me better than to think that."

Okay, take a deep breath and consider whether or not you have ever made an honest mistake in dealing with a friend. Even good friends have momentary lapses of good judgment, and the Bible tells us that no man is above sin. If she believes you have committed a wrong against her, then she should bring it up. If she is wrong, you will have the opportunity to clear up any misconceptions concerning the situation.

"She shouldn't be coming to me with these issues."

If we're honest with ourselves, we'd admit that this statement is rooted in pride. To say that a friend whom we've entrusted with our life cannot come to us with an issue is absurd. It denotes that we believe we are above correction or even worse above her. Allow her to share her concerns then address it. Otherwise, the lines of communication will be shut down, and the relationship will suffer from it.

If you have believed any of the statements above, recondition your mind to be open to listening to your friend's offense. Consider the alternative: if she doesn't present the problem, Satan could play on her thoughts and lead her to believe something concerning you that is not true. If she expresses the concern and there is some falsehood in it, Satan's lies would be exposed. I'll take a moment of conversational discomfort any day instead of the alternative.

CHAPTER 10

Competition

*It's true that some are preaching out of jealousy and rivalry.
But others preach about Christ with pure motives. They preach
because they love me, for they know I have been appointed to
defend the Good News. Those others do not have pure motives
as they preach about Christ. They preach with selfish
ambition, not sincerely, intending to make my chains more
painful to me. -Philippians 1:15-17*

It's no surprise that one of the top challenges in
female friendships is competition. If you take a look at
our society, you will find that women are often put in
positions to compare themselves with other women.
Magazines report which woman wore the same outfit
best. Social media sites constantly report who's
trending and who has the most followers. The
entertainment industry has multiple categories to
indicate which female artist is the best out of the rest.
Then you have male dominated job markets that
force the few women in them to compete for top spots.
Competition is all around us, and if we are not
careful, we can allow it to destroy our relationships.
Anything that rises up a desire in us to perform better
than the person next to us is rooted in pride, not God.

I'm not talking about a friendly family game where someone has to come out the winner. I'm talking about when a person takes that friendly family game and purposely turns it into a bloodbath. I'm referring to the type of unhealthy competition that leads a person to go out of her way to trump or look better than others.

Lifeline: *Anything that rises up a desire in us to perform better than the person next to us is rooted in pride, not God.*

Within friendship circles, it's often subtle. It doesn't parade itself around. There's no verbal announcement of its presence. It's simply a small comment or gesture that leaves the other person involved dumbfounded. Among women, it's often in the form of one-upping. One-upping occurs when an individual presents or accomplishes something good that another friend in the same circle later replicates. That person then goes and does it slightly better to be seen as the more accomplished person.

One study participant, Amber, experienced this as the lead teacher in her classroom. Whenever she presented a lesson to her assistant, the assistant would then take the lesson and find something similar that she felt was better. If the class received any recognition, the assistant would seek to take the credit. A while later, Amber purchased a new car. Upon seeing it, her assistant went out and bought a newer vehicle and made it known to others that she purchased it simply because Amber had.

Sara also experienced one-upping when she received an expensive purse from her father. After showing it to her friends, one of them went out and bought the same bag along with the billfold to go along with it. Dominique, on the other hand, purchased a 32" inch flat screen television. After seeing it, her friend went out and bought a larger version of the same electronic.

One-upping can also occur in circles of mothers who compete to make their child look the best. Hannah, in a moment of excitement and joy, spoke of her son's school accomplishment to a group of friends. After doing so, another mother chimed in and indicated that her child did the same thing at a younger age. In another instance, one mother placed her child in a highly ranked school after finding out that a friend's daughter was going to a school that was also considered to be good. Similar experiences also show up in the way a mother dresses her child or does his or her hair. However, the underlying factor is always the same: to be seen as better than others.

If left unchecked, unhealthy competition will lead to the death of a friendship. It may seem harmless at first, but if you allow it to continue, it will turn into an untamed fire leaving nothing but destruction. Take Pam for example. Pam had been close friends with

Kelsey for years. As time passed, Kelsey began to make new friends who were complete opposites of Pam. As the group began spending more time together, Pam and the others began to compete for Kelsey's affection. After a while, each one would become jealous if another spent time alone with her. At the height of the competition, one of the girls pushed Pam out of the way to sit next to Kelsey. The competition eventually drove Pam away from the group as well as her friend Kelsey.

If you are experiencing competition in friendships, know that there is hope. The disciples themselves struggled with competition. They argued over who in the group of twelve was the greatest (Mark 9:33-35). The mother of James and John even asked if her sons could sit next to Jesus in Heaven. I imagine that the other 10 rolled their eyes at that request (Matthew 20:20-24). However, Jesus responded with the explanation that in order to be the greatest, you have to serve others and become what it considered to be the least. Despite their struggles, the disciples went on to become successful in spreading the gospel of Christ across many nations because at some point they stopped being concerned about being the best in the group. Their focus shifted from competing to aiding and encouraging one another to complete the task at hand. It's no different for us today. In order to become great, we must humble ourselves and serve others. We are most like Jesus when we reach out to help others, not trump them. As members of one body in Christ, we must recognize that the success of one member is a victory for us all.

Lifeline: We are most like Jesus when we reach out to help others not trump them.

CHAPTER 11
The Issue of Trust

Even my best friend, the one I trusted completely, the one who shared my food, has turned against me. -Psalms 41:9

Have you ever shared something confidential with someone only to find out later that she shared that bit of information with others? Or found out that someone you trusted has been lying to you or is not the person you thought she was? If not, thank God for sparing you from such circumstances or giving you a considerable amount of discernment to be able to avoid it. I haven't always been quite as discerning, and I'll tell you from experience that it is not a good feeling. Afterward, there is a dangerous yet natural inclination not to trust those around you. You begin to wonder if others will betray you at some point. However, one person breaking your trust doesn't mean that all others will as well. Continuing to entertain such thoughts spurs on suspicion and leads to superficial or destroyed friendships. To combat those thoughts follow the advice written by the Apostle Paul in Philippians 4:8 "And now, dear brothers and sisters, one final thing. Fix your thoughts on what is true, and honorable, and right, and pure, and lovely, and admirable. Think about things that are excellent and worthy of praise." Ask yourself if it's true that everyone in your life will at some point betray you? Is it honorable or admirable to think so? Framing your thoughts in the context of this scripture will help combat irrational thinking. Healthy relationships cannot exist with such thoughts. Trust has to be the foundation, or the relationship will collapse.

Where does it all begin?

The battle to trust others often starts when the person who has broken our trust is a close friend or relative. Ahithophel, for example, was the trusted and well-respected advisor to King David. He is the familiar friend that David speaks of in Psalm 41 and 55. The two enjoyed a close friendship and often walked together to the house of God. David sought his counsel because he was known for his good judgment and keen discernment. He was a leader, and when he spoke, people listened. Interestingly enough the name Ahithophel means brother of insipidity or one who lacks reverence or interest.[11] This proved to be true when King David's son, Absalom, sought to take the throne from him. He called for Ahithophel who agreed to go along with him as his new advisor. The news devastated King David. However, it didn't prevent him from trusting those around him who remained faithful, and it shouldn't prevent us either.

How do I go about trusting others?

Trusting others will always be a risk because it requires that we become vulnerable to them. While we can't prevent others from hurting us, we can use wisdom in when and how we go about trusting others. A person should always earn you trust over time with experience. Jesus didn't blindly trust others and neither should we (John 2:23). The Apostle Paul even encouraged Timothy to study and show himself approved by God (2 Timothy 2:15). If God looks at our actions before giving approval, then surely we should follow in His footsteps and do the same.

Lifeline: Jesus didn't blindly trust others and neither should we.

Several years ago, my husband and I were in a transitioning stage in our lives. I felt God leading me to step down from certain roles in my church as well as my full-time job outside the church. When I shared the scripture and personal direction that God had given me with someone I considered to be a friend; the person was discouraging and condescending. After the conversation, I came to realize that each time I had shared something personal with this individual, I experienced the same result. My hope of having this person as a close friend clouded my ability to see that she was not someone I needed to trust with the intimate details of my life. Although she possessed many admirable qualities, our interactions proved that she wasn't to be a trusted confidante for me. The initial disappointment of my deflated hope stung. But as I sat in the middle of my new reality, I began to realize that if God wasn't orchestrating an intimate friendship with this person, then I shouldn't be pushing for it either.

Don't allow your desire to be close to someone overcrowd good judgment. Slowly become acquainted with her and take note of your interactions with one another. Ask yourself if she has proven to be the person that she has presented over time. Does she keep her word and honor her commitments? If so, gradually begin to share more information with her. Then, continue to watch her actions. If she happens to reveal a confidence, break a commitment, or respond in a negative way, note how she responds when you bring it to her attention. Does she admit her mistake and seek to correct it or does she continue to make the same mistakes over and over? A friend that admits her mistakes and changes afterward is worthy of your trust. A person that glosses over her mistakes and continues to make them is questionable. If this is the case, discontinue sharing information with her until you see her actions change.

What should I do after a friend has destroyed my trust?

In situations where someone has earned your trust then betrays it, pray. Be honest with God about how you feel no matter how ugly it may be. He will not strike you down, and He won't be shocked by any of your thoughts and feelings because He already knows them. Remember to reverence Him as God but be honest. This will begin the healing process and invite God to work in your situation. King David used the same strategy in his prayers. The book of Psalms displays many of these examples. If you take a look at chapter 55, you'll find that David did not spare God of his feelings concerning Ahithophel. He was open and honest about it, but he didn't stop there. He then shifted his attention on the character of God and remembered all of God's promises toward him. In all of your communications with God, you should do the same. As far as trusting that person again with personal or confidential matters, use good judgment. The previous guidelines should apply. Did she admit her mistake and seek to correct it? Does her current track record prove that she has changed? If not, stop sharing confidential or personal information until you see her actions change.

CHAPTER 12
Betrayal

For it is not an enemy who taunts me—then I could bear it; it is not an adversary who deals insolently with me—then I could hide from him. But it is you, a man, my equal, my companion, my familiar friend. -Psalm 55:12-13 ESV

Although betrayal was not one of the top five challenges, it frequently comes up when talking about female friendships. Its appearance in a person's life is strongly noted and leaves a lasting impression afterward. If you've never experienced the slap of betrayal, there is nothing quite like it. The initial shock stops you dead in your tracks and causes you to gasp for air. Your heartbeat races and your breathing speeds up as you try to regain composure and make sense of it all. As reality begins to sink in, your mind races and your memory becomes amazingly clear. You start to see all the warning signs laid before you. You ask yourself how you could have possibly missed them. Perhaps it's because it's at the hand of someone you trusted or loved deeply. In fact, a betrayal can only occur if an individual has earned your trust or there has been a pledge to loyalty. Betrayal by definition is any unexpected act that violates trust. It can include a list of things such as revealing personal information to a friend's enemy or refusing to submit to inappropriate expectations of a close friend.

In the middle of the most challenging time of his life, Job bore his soul to his friends (See Job 1-25). The Lord had allowed Satan to test Job's faithfulness to Him by first destroying all his earthly possessions including his children. When Job received news that a series of events destroyed everything he had, he proved his faithfulness by falling down on his face and worshipping God. Afterward, Satan reappeared before God and requested to test Job's faithfulness again by attacking his health. God granted the request and Job was struck with sores from the top of his head to the soles of his feet. As word spread of Job's demise, three of his friends arranged to go and comfort him. When they arrived and realized the magnitude of his suffering, they mourned and sat in silence with him for seven days and seven nights. Afterward, Job spoke openly and frankly about the situation. Unfortunately, Job's friends responded to his honesty with insults. They too spoke candidly, but their words pierced and tormented Job's soul. As Job sat racked with physical and emotional pain, his closest friends uttered the following:

- You are guilty of sin
- Those who are immoral and create trouble will reap it

- The Lord revealed to me that you are guilty
- You need to repent
- You don't fear God
- You deserve worse
- Your wickedness is great
- God punishes the wicked, and they will suffer

It was horrible and gives a whole new perspective to kicking a man when he's down. His friends, who had journeyed to comfort him, had now begun attacking him. They made it a point to try and convince him that he was wicked. Based on Job 1:8, Job was found to be blameless. God says of Job in that verse "...there is none like him on the earth, a blameless and upright man, who fears God and turns away from evil" (ESV)? However, his friends thought otherwise.

> ***They confronted me in the day of my calamity, but the Lord was my support.***
> ***-Psalms 18:18 ESV***

Many of us have experienced something similar. We've shared personal struggles with friends only to walk away more discouraged than when we came. We've trusted others with confidential information only to find she's taken that information and shared it with others. We've had friends turn others against us and in some cases, sleep with a significant other. No matter what the situation, the result always leads to heartache. If we are not careful, we can allow that heartache to get the best of us. Holding on to it leads to unforgiveness which in turn allows bitterness to take root causing all kinds of rotten fruit. However, handing it over to the Lord allows Him to not only save us but to heal our broken hearts.

> **The LORD is near to the brokenhearted and saves the crushed in spirit. -Psalm 34:18 ESV**

So how do we hand it over? After the initial shock wears off, pray. This will position you to receive strength and direction from God concerning what to do next. Specifically, ask God whether or not you should continue in a close relationship with the person. He is faithful to answer and will show you what to do next. In Job's case, God told him to pray for his friends. The Bible does not indicate whether or not they continued to be close, but it does explain that Job went on to lead a great life. After praying, God blessed him and gave him twice as much as he had before. He went on to have ten more children including three daughters who were considered to be the most beautiful in the land. He lived an additional 140 years and saw four generations after him. His journey was not an easy one, and it won't be for us either. Despite your feelings, choose to forgive and submit those who betray you to prayer. Doing so allows the Lord to heal your heart and bless you with more than you had before.

Types of betrayal

Although betrayals come in many forms, they all fall into two categories: betrayals with cause or betrayals without cause. In Psalm 7:3-5 David brings this notion to light. In it, he says, "O Lord my God, if I have done wrong or am guilty of injustice, if I have betrayed a friend or plundered my enemy without cause, then let my enemies capture me." David was obviously confident that he was innocent of such charges, but he brings up an excellent point. There are times when betrayals become necessary. Remember, a betrayal is any act that violates another person's trust in you. It is not necessarily a malicious act performed to inflict harm. Many situations can lead to a break in trust with another individual. For instance, if a person trusts you with confidential information that will bring harm to herself or others, a betrayal becomes necessary. If a person expects you to assist her in any illegal or immoral activity, a betrayal becomes necessary. If a person becomes abusive then no longer trusts you when you attempt to establish boundaries, then betrayal becomes necessary. Don't allow others to condemn you in these type situations. It is absolutely necessary to break trust. In some cases, you must part company with the individual. This is what I refer to as a betrayal with cause.

A betrayal without cause would be any preventable act that violates a person's trust. A perfect example can be found in the movie *The Women* when the main character, Mary, goes through an unexpected separation with her husband. After finding out about his infidelity, Mary contacts her best friend, Sylvie, who is working her dream job as the editor-in-chief of a magazine. Unfortunately, the magazine is failing, and her dream job is on the line. Out of desperation, Sylvie gives all the details of Mary's divorce to a gossip columnist in an attempt to save her job. The journalist later publishes the story, and Sylvie reveals her betrayal. However, the betrayal was completely preventable which makes it a betrayal without cause. Betrayals only become necessary when a person requires that you compromise your character, values, safety, or most importantly your walk with God. Otherwise, they are unacceptable and cause unnecessary damage to both parties involved.

Lifeline: Betrayals only become necessary when a person requires that you compromise your character, values, safety, or most importantly your walk with God.

What do I do after I have betrayed a friend?

If you are the person who has committed a

betrayal without cause, confess it as sin and repent. 1 John 1:9 tells us "If we confess our sins, he is faithful and just to forgive us our sins and to cleanse us from all unrighteousness." Trust that God has forgiven you of the offense and don't allow the Enemy to condemn you concerning it. Then, earnestly seek to apologize and make things right with the person. Do not, however, attempt to make her forgive you. Your job is to walk in love towards her regardless of her actions. You should also come to terms with the fact that an apology does not mean she should continue in a close relationship with you. Restoration can only take place if you have regained her trust. You will only regain her trust if your actions reflect that you are truly repentant. This takes place over an extended period of time. However, it still does not guarantee that you will become close friends again. Pray for God to heal both of your hearts concerning any pain caused by your actions. Then, be open to God's will for you concerning the type of relationship you should have with the person in the future.

CHAPTER 13
Letting Go & Bidding Adieu

For everything there is a season, and a time for every matter under heaven: ...a time to seek, and a time to lose; a time to keep, and a time to cast away. -Ecclesiastes 3:1,6 (ESV)

I was in the middle of a mess. I had just finished one of those uncomfortable conversations addressing an issue I had with a friend. Weeks had passed before I gathered up the courage to talk to her about it. I mulled over the situation numerous times trying to tuck it into some form of acceptable practice. Each time I thought of it I had a gnawing feeling in the pit of my stomach. The issue had become a stumbling block for me in the relationship, and I needed to address it. I nervously dialed her number and carefully explained my thoughts and feelings concerning the situation. Unfortunately, the conversation did not go well. By the time I hung up, I was upset and in complete shock over what had taken place. "Surely, this is a mistake," I thought but it wasn't. Days later I received a message indicating the friendship was over. Although I was hurt, I respected the decision. I later received an apology and accepted, but the entire situation left me feeling uneasy. I needed space to pray, think, and hear from God. Then, after fasting, I received clear instructions from the Lord: I needed to walk away. I didn't know all the ins and outs of why. I didn't even believe she was out to hurt me, but I did have enough reverential fear of God to trust His direction. So I took my exit and as weeks passed, the Lord reaffirmed His instruction through various bible studies. It became more and more evident why I needed to walk away. Despite this confirmation, the pain of the separation became distracting. I didn't begin to snap out of it until the Lord personally told to me that He could not use me to help others if I was always focusing on myself. Focusing on a relationship that the Lord is leading you to walk away from will inevitably lead to hindered purpose.

Lifeline: Focusing on a relationship that the Lord is leading you to walk away from will inevitably lead to hindered purpose.

Take Abram for example. When God first spoke to Abram and told him to leave his hometown, He also told him to leave behind his family (See Genesis 12-14). However, when Abram departs, he takes his nephew Lot along with him. Arguments begin to break out between the herdsmen of the two men. To prevent further problems, Abram persuades Lot to go in a different direction, and he departs to a land called Sodom. After his departure, the land is plundered by neighboring kings and Lot is taken captive. When word of Lot's condition reaches Abram, he gathers his trained men and goes to war with the kings. After successfully retrieving his nephew along with all his possessions, the Lord reveals to Abram (now known as Abraham) that He will destroy the very town that Lot calls home. Abraham becomes distraught and begins to bargain with God to spare the city. Ultimately the Lord saves Lot and his family but destroys the town because of its great wickedness. Abraham rises early the next morning and witnesses the smoke rising from the city. His eagerness to see its condition is an indicator that he had an emotional investment in Lot. I believe it is this investment that prevented him from fully following the Lord's instruction. As a result, he became distracted from his purpose. Instead of focusing on what God was leading him to do, time was wasted settling disputes, fighting a war, and being in heartache over a city the Lord set out to destroy. Abraham could have prevented a lot of problems had he listened and taken his God-given exit.

I won't bother to tell you that walking away from someone you love and once trusted is easy. It's not. In fact, breaking up with a friend can be extremely difficult because of the emotional investment. In the book Toxic Friends by Susan Shapiro Barash, Dr. Donald Cohen puts it this way: "When something goes awry with a close female friend, it's emotionally charged. Only breaking up a family due to divorce is more devastating."[12] It's not a task anyone would enjoy doing, but sometimes, it is necessary. Oftentimes our emotional ties and personal misconceptions prevent us from letting go. For me that misconception concerned loyalty. I was of the mindset that every friend in my life would be there forever. As a result, I kept close ties to unhealthy relationships long after the warning signs appeared. I lacked the understanding that loyalty becomes dangerous when it puts you in a position of losing yourself to pacify others.

Lifeline: *Loyalty becomes dangerous when it puts you in a position of losing yourself to pacify others.*

Recognizing the warning signs

The Lord will always give clear warning signs of a bad relationship. However, our emotional ties can prevent us from identifying them. Unfortunately, they also prevent us from seeing the damaging effects of that relationship. Because these friendships have such an impact on our health and life purposes, it is important to recognize the warning signs of a bad relationship. If you take a close look at a person's actions, the truth becomes more evident.

In the movie *Little Black Book*, a talk show producer

named Barb cons the new employee, Stacy, into digging into her boyfriend's past.[13] Throughout the film, she consistently plants seeds of distrust and encourages her to find out more and more information concerning his ex-girlfriends. Barb later reveals that she was using Stacy to create a grand finale for the show. Ironically after setting her plan into motion, Barb says to Stacy "People will tell you who they are if you just listen." Had Stacy realized the magnitude of that statement, she could've saved herself some heartache. So pay close attention, not only to a person's words but more importantly to her actions. Ask yourself the following questions:

- Does this person continuously distract me from my God-given purpose?
- Do I compromise my relationship with Christ when I'm around this person?
- Is the friendship one-sided? Am I consistently giving more than I am receiving?
- Is she physically, verbally, or emotionally abusive?
- Does she willingly expose me to dangerous situations?
- Am I consistently drained physically, emotionally, or spiritually after spending time with this person?

If you answered yes to any of the questions above, it

serves as a warning to step back from the relationship. Do not brush it aside or ignore it. Take heed to the Lord's warnings with the understanding that it is for your own good and ignoring them will be to your detriment. Don't fool yourself into thinking the person is someone other than who they have shown themselves to be over time. Consider Proverbs 27:19 which reads "As in water face reflects face, so the heart of man reflects the man." Take that reflection at face value then seek God's will as to how to interact with that person in the future.

As you begin to step back, beware of the Enemy's tactics to guilt you into remaining in the bad relationship. If you are in a position of physical, emotional, or spiritual harm, you should remove yourself. Jesus himself practiced this behavior before the crucifixion. In Luke 4:28-30, Jesus removed himself from a crowd that desired to push Him over a ledge. John 10:31-39 gives an account of Jesus removing himself after a crowd sought to stone Him. Matthew 12:13-15 shows Jesus leaving an area after becoming aware of the Pharisee's plot to kill Him. Jesus did not willing remain in situations where people sought to do Him harm before His appointed time. When that time came, He permitted it for the sole purpose of making all humanity right with God again. It is never God's will for you to allow someone to abuse you for the sake of her well-being. Step away from the situation and allow God to heal you heart concerning it.

If it is the Lord's will to bring you back together, He will do it within His timing and provide clear instructions concerning it. Until then steer clear of any relationship the Lord instructs you to release.

CHAPTER 14
Moving Forward

Therefore, since we are surrounded by so great a cloud of witnesses, let us also lay aside every weight, and sin which clings so closely, and let us run with endurance the race that is set before us, -Hebrews 12:1 ESV

After betrayals, broken trust, and bad departures have taken place, you'll have to fight the urge to withdraw from current friendships or avoid new ones altogether. In order to maintain or establish healthy friendships, trust has to be the foundation. To prevent any root of bitterness from springing up, you must forgive the ones who have betrayed you or even departed from your life. The Bible very clearly instructs us to forgive and walk in love towards one another. But what does that mean and how do we practice it in everyday life?

In Matthew 18:21-22, Peter asks Jesus how many times he must forgive his brother. The Greek word for forgive in this passage is aphiémi which means to lay aside, leave alone, or let go.[14] Peter was well versed in the religious law and would have known at the time of his question that forgiving someone up to three times was the religious custom. He probably assumed that his suggestion of seven was more than fair. However, Jesus responds by instructing Peter to forgive his brother 70 times seven. A number that would be nearly impossible to keep up with. However, his response brings about two interesting points. The first being that in order to consciously forgive someone 490 times, you must first have a memory of the previous 489 offenses. While God has the ability to forgive and forget our sins (Isaiah 43:25 & Hebrews 8:12), He did not construct our human minds to willfully forget events that are unpleasant. If He did, there would be no need to forgive because we simply would not remember they took place. Not being able to recall a wrong committed against you is not a good indicator of forgiveness nor is it a standard that God requires us to uphold. While there are cases where a person forgives and no longer remembers the incident, it is foolish to place that expectation on fellow believers. For it to hold true, victims of rape or those who have lost a loved one due to a violent crime would have to completely forget the situation took place to forgive the offender. True forgiveness means laying aside a wrong committed with full awareness that it took place.

The second point is that walking in forgiveness can sometimes mean continuously letting go of an offense that only occurred once. This means that every time you remember the incident, you choose to forgive. Consider the number of times you have replayed an offensive situation in your head. If you did not consciously choose to forgive the person the moment you remembered it, you probably became angry and offended all over again. If you're anything like me, you would even contemplate what you should have said that you didn't say in response to their actions. However, when you set your heart to walk in forgiveness continuously, your memory of the event will no longer spark anger. It will not happen overnight but, it will take place eventually.

To be clear, Jesus' instruction to forgive 70 times seven is not so much about the number as it is the principle. We know this because of the scripture in 1 Corinthians 13:5 that states that love keeps no records of wrong. The take home point Jesus is making here is that forgiveness is a regular way of life, not a one-time deal. To live a life of forgiveness, you must fully acknowledge the hurt then continuously choose to lay it aside for your good. It does not mean that what the person did was okay. It also doesn't mean that we must act as if it never happened. Forgiveness does not give the person a pass for their bad behavior. It is instead a conscious choice to trust God to handle the situation instead of taking the matter into your hands.

What does forgiveness look like in everyday life?

Oftentimes what hinders me from immediately forgiving others is my emotions. There is no doubt in my mind that the Lord wants me to forgive but when I take my feelings into consideration, I delay my obedience. While God gives you emotions and they are not evil, they can sometimes deceive and steer you in the wrong direction if they lead you to do what is contrary to the word of God. According to the word, you should not let the sun go down on our anger or the devil will gain access into your life (Ephesians 4:26-27). If you wait until we feel like forgiving others, you may never get around to it, and the devil could wreak havoc. It's a risk we cannot afford to take. When we make a conscious choice to forgive, our feelings will eventually follow suit.

In my daily interactions, that means choosing not to retaliate when someone gives an insult or belittling comment. It means not seeking to destroy a person's reputation, but to live in peace with others and to pray for them even if I don't feel like it. Why? Because forgiveness is a choice, not a feeling. Jesus instructed us to love and pray for those who mistreat us. He even goes on to say to greet them (Matthew 5:44-47). Solely greeting and acting in love towards those who love us is a worldly concept. It may not always be easy but, God enables us to do it through the power of the Holy Spirit.

Lifeline: Forgiveness is a choice, not a feeling.

The example of Jesus

As believers, we should always take our cue of how to interact with others from Jesus and the scriptures. During the most difficult time of His life, Jesus demonstrated what it looks like to forgive. Peter testifies of this in 1 Peter 2:23 indicating "He did not retaliate when he was insulted, nor threaten revenge when he suffered. He left his case in the hands of God, who always judges fairly." This reminder was a guideline for Peter's fellow believers exiled in foreign lands. Jesus served as the perfect example as they experienced harsh criticisms and sufferings due to their faith. His response while standing trial before the high priest and Pilate is nothing short of remarkable (Mark 14:55-61, Mark15:1-20). While the religious leaders hurled insults and false accusations towards Him, Jesus remained silent. As soldiers insulted and mocked Him, Jesus refused to react. Surely, as the son of God, He would have been justified in His response. Still, He chose to trust God with the situation instead.

1 Peter 3:9 encourages us to do the same. In it, we are instructed "Don't repay evil for evil. Don't retaliate with insults when people insult you. Instead, pay them back with a blessing. That is what God has called you to do, and he will grant you his blessing." Although it is a tall order, God's will for us is to trust Him when others treat us poorly. His word promises us that He will take care of the situation (Romans

12:19). Therefore, it is not necessary to retaliate. Trusting God with the situation is the only step you need to take.

Forgiving Close Friends

When the person you need to forgive is a trusted friend the command to forgive may become a little more challenging. The existence of close ties can deceptively lead one to assume the other person would never do anything hurtful. The Bible warns us that no man is above sin (Ecclesiastes 7:20). Therefore, it is possible for even our closest friends to let us down or hurt us. So how do you handle those upsets? Let's take another look at Jesus. While praying in one of His most common hang out spots, His disciple, Judas, hand delivered Him into the care of His enemies (Matthew 26:50). Although Jesus acknowledges the betrayal, He makes no attempt to retaliate. Nor does he hurl insults or give death stares. There was no public denouncement of Judas or declaration of the wrong committed. He submitted to God's plan with no attempted vengeance.

After this incident, one would think that matters couldn't get any worse in the friend's department. However, immediately following Jesus' arrest, the remaining disciples deserted Him. Peter, one of Jesus' closest friends who declared he'd die with Him, denies even knowing Him. But Jesus full of grace and mercy reappears to the remaining disciples. He makes a conscious choice to not only forgive but continue walking with the very friends that betrayed Him. Recall that before any of this happened, Jesus spent an entire night in prayer selecting these men. Therefore, it is of the utmost importance that you pray and seek God about your relationships as well. This allowed Jesus to receive a clear directive from God concerning them.

Despite this directive, there was still a critical factor that played into Peter's restoration. After his denial, Peter wept bitterly over what he had done, but that was not enough. Luke 22:31-32 records Jesus instructing Peter to repent and turn towards Him again. Only then would he be able to rejoin his brothers and strengthen them. Thankfully, the account in Mark 16:7 displays an angel instructing Mary Magdalene to go and tell the disciples, including Peter, that Jesus had resurrected from the dead. The angel's particular reference to Peter indicates that he had returned to the remaining disciples. To do so, he must have followed the directive of Jesus to repent (turn in the opposite direction) of his actions. True repentance must be present before restoration takes place.

While there are no cookie cutter answers as to whether or not you should continue in a close friendship with someone who has betrayed you, you should consider the following questions:

- Does she acknowledge or deny the wrongdoing?
- Does she apologize or make excuses?
- Does she accept responsibility or blame you?
- Does she profess to make changes or see nothing wrong with her behavior?
- Does she speak from a place of love or hatred?

Your answers will shed some light on how to proceed. Do not continue in a close relationship with someone who does not acknowledge any wrongdoing and persists in the same negative pattern of behavior. As you pray and seek God for the direction of the relationship in the future, remember that we are always commanded to forgive and walk in love towards others. This means you must resist the urge to retaliate and trust God to handle the situation.

CHAPTER 15
Iron Sharpening Iron

As iron sharpens iron, so a friend sharpens a friend.
-Proverbs 27:17

A good friend of mine called to check in on me as she often does. On this particular day, I happened to be in the middle of a terrible situation. I had commenced throwing myself a pretty awesome pity party and thought to extend her an invitation. She knew nothing of the ordeal, so I began to inform her of my current events. Just as I began to extend my invitation, she interrupted me and said, "You have to forgive." She then proceeded to explain how I'm hurting myself by not forgiving and what a joy it would be if I did. As anyone could imagine, it ruined my pity party. I wanted to tell my full story and have her sympathize with me. I wanted her to join me in my pity party and pacify me. But anyone with a real truth-telling friend can tell you she didn't. The likelihood of her doing so in the future is slim to none. Instead, I got a heaping dose of the pure, unadulterated truth. It wasn't rude. It wasn't mean. It was what I needed to hear at the time to become better. Her actions as Proverbs 27:17 describes helped sharpen me.

I wish I could tell you that I enjoyed this sharpening session at the time but I didn't. I liken it to being in the middle of an intense workout. Usually, at that point, I've convinced myself the trainer is crazy, and I'm going to die. I begin to seriously consider stopping to alleviate the pain and prevent any premature meeting with Jesus. However, once the workout is over and I actually see results, the pain becomes worth it, and the trainer and I are once again on good terms.

Friendships are very similar. Some points are painful, but they help you grow. To become better, you have to have at least one friend that can help sharpen you. If you're not sure if you have one, ask yourself the following questions. Do I have a friend that:

- Tells me the truth even if it's not in her favor to do so
- Challenges me to do my very best
- Leads me to think or look at things from a different perspective
- Corrects me when I'm wrong and still loves me afterward

If you answered yes to the questions above, thank God for giving you an iron sharpening friend. Not having this type of relationship is dangerous.

Surrounding yourself with people who only tell you what you want to hear will hurt you. Having my friend speak the truth helped snap me out of my pity mode and realize that in order to get over the situation, I had to stop feeling sorry for myself. The funny thing is, I love her more for telling me the truth instead of pacifying my feelings. In the end, it was well worth it. But when you're going through an iron sharpening session, there are a few things you should keep in mind.

Whenever things become intense during one of my workouts, I always remember the trainer's promise of results and her instruction never to stop moving. If the workout becomes too intense, I can always slow down so long as I continue with the exercise and refuse to stop moving. Completely stopping when I become uncomfortable prevents me from getting the results I want. In friendships, the same principle holds true. When a friend who has proven to have your best interest in mind offers unsolicited wise counsel, remember that she desires to help you, not hurt you. Even if it's too much to handle at the moment, take some time to process the information then keep moving forward. Her courage to speak the truth can save you a lot of time, effort, money, and heartache. It is better to hear a friend's thoughts concerning a pending mistake before suffering the consequences of that decision. Hearing of it afterward is not beneficial to anyone.

Lifeline: When a friend who has proven to have your best interest in mind offers unsolicited wise counsel, remember that she desires to help you, not hurt you.

If you struggle to tell your friends the truth, remember it is to her benefit. She may not like it at the moment or even appreciate your courage to say it. However, once her emotions die down and she logically processes the information, she will likely appreciate the fact that you care. Consider how the woman caught in the act of adultery must have felt (John 8:1-11). After being pardoned from death, she stood face to face with Jesus. As the reality of what had just taken place began to sink in, Jesus responded with love and honesty. His love compelled Him to pardon her from death, but His honesty led Him to plainly tell her to stop sinning. There was no condemnation or guilt trip concerning her actions. But He also didn't attempt to make her feel better about the situation or offer advice on how to not get caught the next time. I imagine after coming close to being stoned, the woman was emotionally vulnerable. The day's events probably caused her to feel an array of emotions: from fear to elation to remorse. That did not stop Jesus from telling her the truth. Even in her vulnerable emotional state, do you think she was more concerned about Jesus telling her the truth or the fact that He cared enough to find a way to pardon her from it? Even if Jesus' statement to stop sinning hurt her feelings, she probably appreciated it in the end. Hopefully, your friends will too.

In offering advice to a friend, keep in mind the scriptures do not give you license to unload negative criticism or force others to live up to your personal standards. The standard as believers is and always will be Jesus Christ. If you offer any correction or unsolicited advice to your friends, base it on the word of God. Your personal opinions should never be used to govern the lives of others.

CHAPTER 16

Maintaining the Gold

So in everything, do to others what you would have them do to you, for this sums up the Law and the Prophets.
-Matthew 7:12 NIV

It's tempting to look at a friendship from the outside and assume that those involved never experience challenges. The devil would love for us to believe that others have it easy in this department and never experience the heartaches and disappointments that we do. However, after talking to over 100 women, I can tell you that the battle wages for all of us. We each experience disappointments and get upset with our best friends. Walking away from these relationships can be tempting. However, if the person embodies the qualities you desire in a friend and has proven to have your best interest in mind, resist the urge to blacklist her and find a new group of friends. Just as in those tough workouts, keep the friendship moving. Then follow the directive of Jesus in Matthew 7:12 (also known as The Golden Rule). In it, He gives an instruction to treat others the way you desire for them to treat you. When we hold up this passage against our circumstance, it becomes easier to see how we should respond in tough situations. If your friend has said something hurtful, imagine the roles reversed. How would you want her to respond if you said something hurtful to her? If she missed an important event or failed to support you in some way, put yourself in her shoes. Would you want her to accuse you of being a poor friend or check and see if everything is okay? Even if you find her reason to be unacceptable, place yourself in her position. Doing so makes it easier to extend grace and forgiveness which will come in handy when, not if, the tables turn. I can't tell you the number of times I've said something foolish or failed to support a friend in some way. Often it was because I didn't recognize the significance of the event or the impact of my words. Addressing the problem brings about awareness and opens a door of opportunity for individual growth as well as growth in the friendship. We all want others to think the best of us and extend forgiveness. Therefore, we should think the best of others and forgive them as well.

Lifeline: If the person embodies the qualities you desire in a friend and has proven to have your best interest in mind, resist the urge to blacklist her and find a new group of friends.

In your daily interactions with friends, you should always consider the Golden Rule. To have relationships that are loving, supportive, loyal, and honest, your actions towards others must be loving, supportive, loyal, and honest. Likewise, if you want your friends to celebrate your accomplishments and show up to major life events, then you must show up and celebrate their lives as well. On the other hand, if you feel that a request is too much to ask of you, then that same request is too much to ask of your friends. Your expectations of others must be the standard by which you live. Otherwise, it will be hard to maintain trust which is the foundation of every healthy friendship. Think about it. What happens when a person who regularly calls on you for support rarely returns the favor? After a certain amount of time, you will likely begin to question her trustworthiness and distance yourself. Don't put others in that position. Create stability in the relationship by maintaining your own personal standards. Once you establish that standard, you can begin focusing on another important aspect of maintaining friendships: looking towards the interests of others.

In every relationship I have, I ask myself how I can add value. The answer to the question always depends on the person's individual interests as well as her circumstances. Paul and Timothy spoke of this in their letter to the church in Philippi. In it, they advised the church members to not only look out for their own interest but towards the interest of others as well (Philippians 2:4). In order to do so, we must humble ourselves and consider what is best for the other person. Take your best friend, for example. What are her personal interests, goals, and needs at the moment? Consider ways to support her in those areas. If she is stepping out and trying something new, you can offer support through prayer or give a word of encouragement. If she's starting a new business, you can show support by purchasing the product, telling others about her business, or lending a helping hand. If she has a new addition to her family, you can offer support by taking a meal or helping with the housework. If you are not sure what her interests or needs are at the moment, begin to actively listen when she speaks. Then pray for ways to help her in those areas. When you feel prompted to encourage her in some way, do it. That is the leading of the Holy Spirit and the answer to your prayer. I guarantee you if the Holy Spirit leads you to do it, it will help her as well as cause the friendship to grow. However, remember to keep it simple. Try to remain as practical as possible. The action does not have to be elaborate or extravagant to be effective. The goal is to add value to the friendship. Adding value does not necessarily mean spending a lot of time or money, but it will take effort.

My sister, Rochelle, is constantly looking towards the interest of others and is a prime example of what it means to be supportive. Two years ago her best friend, Sabrina, was diagnosed with stage 4 colon cancer. They met and quickly became acquainted in high school and remained close over the years. Because of the nature of the disease, Sabrina immediately began medical treatments which included an extensive surgery and travel out of town for specialist care. Through it all, my sister stood by her side. She made trips to the hospital and traveled out of town for some of her treatments. When Sabrina became nauseous to the point of vomiting, Rochelle held her container. Often during the weekends, she would pick up Sabrina's son who was ten days older than her daughter. He spent time with her family and quickly became a part of it. Her actions were completely selfless. She could have cited her family and work as reasons not to look towards the interest of Sabrina. Instead, she remained supportive until the very end. Sabrina eventually died of complications from cancer. Even after her death, Rochelle continued to look towards Sabrina's interest. She helped the family plan the funeral and vowed to care for Sabrina's son as if he were her own. To this day, I get photo texts of their children playing together. It is a reminder to me of what it means to take an interest in others.

If you have anything close to a friend like Rochelle, show your appreciation for her. Many things that demand our time and attention. Having someone take a break from her busy schedule to listen, encourage, pray, or spend time with you is an honor you should not take for granted. The fact that she does so indicates her love for you and the significance of friendship. Let her know she is just as significant and loved by you by looking towards her interests in return. Don't get discouraged if you don't get it right 100% of the time. We are all human. Mistakes are a part of the process. Learn from them then keep moving forward.

CHAPTER 17

Into the New

Can two walk together, except they be agreed? -Amos 3:3 KJV

"I should invite her to lunch," I thought to myself. I had known of this particular person for years but never really got a chance to know her personally. She seemed to be nice and carried herself in a respectful manner. I knew she loved God and served Him faithfully, so I emailed her an invitation to lunch. Afterward, I found myself wondering about all the what ifs. What if she doesn't want to go out to lunch with me? What if we have nothing to talk about when we meet? What if we don't have anything in common and I see her again in public? I began to feel like I was walking into a bad date. My natural tendency to be introverted began to rise. I asked myself "do I really need more friends when I already have a handful?" But, the thought was interrupted by a new set of what ifs. What if I go out to lunch with this person and enjoy her company? What if God put this person in my thoughts to start the beginning of a beautiful friendship? What if this person is supposed to play a vital role in my life? What if I'm meant to play a crucial role in hers? I closed the computer thinking, either way, I would learn from the process. Then woke up the next morning to a message gladly accepting my invitation. My worries of rejection and inadequacy were a waste of time and energy.

Overthinking a potential new friendship can cause you to cheat yourself out of a great experience. Equally frustrating is the tendency to commit to a friendship prematurely which inevitably leads to regret. When a person whom you find to be interesting comes into your life, consider it an opportunity to make a new friend. Resist the urge to label it and fantasize about all the what ifs. Spending time together is not a commitment to friendship. It is a chance to get to know the other person better. Oftentimes, our first glance of an individual is not an accurate picture of a person's real character. It is important to slowly get acquainted with a person before deeming her your friend. Doing so allows you to recognize three factors in determining whether or not to proceed in a friendship. Those three factors include her possession of the biblical qualities of a friend, a shared common interest, and her possession of the qualities you desire in a friend. As previously mentioned the biblical qualities of a friend include:

- Giving wise counsel
- Being an encourager
- Being loving towards others

- Helping others during times of need
- Being slow to anger
- Being trustworthy
- Keeping information confidential

If the person you are spending time with lacks one of three determining factors, it is an indication that there may be a problem. Lacking the qualities of a biblical friend will lead to unnecessary hurt. However, not having a common interest will hinder you from coming together to develop a friendship in the first place. Attempting to establish a relationship with a person who does not have the qualities you need in a friend is a waste of time for everyone involved.

At first glance, it may seem as if lacking one of the biblical qualities is not a big deal but take a closer look. If a person displays most of the biblical qualities but gives unwise counsel, heeding her advice will lead to trouble and cause you to go in a direction that God never intended you to go (Proverbs 13:20 & 12:26). Being friends with someone who is hot tempered will cause you to pick up on her habits and endanger yourself (Proverbs 22:24-25). On the other hand, having a friend who is unable to keep a confidence will lead to shame. If a person you are spending time with lacks any of the biblical qualities, pray for her in that area. Then gracefully take a step back. Having a close, intimate relationship with this person is not a wise decision. It doesn't mean she's a bad person or lacks the potential to be your friend in the future. Nor does it mean you should no longer talk to her. It is instead an indication that she lacks maturity in a vital area of friendship. While none of us are perfect, the deciding factor you are looking at here is whether or not the person habitually practices the negative behavior or is making an honest mistake. Continuing to establish a close relationship with someone who lacks these qualities will lead to pain and regret. However, finding someone who embodies these qualities allows you to move on to a common interest.

A common interest can include anything from being an avid reader to a marathon runner. Having something to draw you together takes away the stress and awkwardness of trying to figure out what to do or talk about when you come together. It will also allow you to do something you both enjoy as you further determine whether or not you want to continue meeting. However, if you find that you don't have any common interests after meeting, you are not obligated to continue establishing a friendship. Friendships consist of mutual love and respect, but there has to be a common interest to draw you two together. Therefore, a person may have the qualities of a biblical friend, but you may not enjoy her company. That's okay. Everyone you come in contact with is not meant to be a close friend. Don't try to force a relationship. At the end of your time together, be honest. Thank her for her time but skip the nicety of suggesting you would like to continue meeting on a regular basis. Perhaps you meet occasionally or have a good conversation whenever you cross paths but don't lead her to think you enjoy her company then cease all communications. Remember the Golden Rule to do unto others as you would have them do unto you. Ask yourself how you would want someone to respond if the tables were turned.

After determining the first two factors of friendships, you can then move on to whether or not the person embodies the qualities you desire in a friend. Most women interviewed wanted those closest to them to be loyal, encouraging, honest, and non-judgmental. They also wanted friends who remained close despite not talking on a daily basis. In considering your personal preferences, determine which qualities are non-negotiable. For instance, two qualities that are important to me are dependability and communication. I want to surround myself with friends whom I can depend on during times of need. I don't call on them often, but when I do, I want them to be there for me. This is not negotiable. On the other hand, frequency and mode of communication are flexible. I prefer to communicate via text for incidental matters and by phone for anything else. However, I have a friend that does not like texting and communicates by phone more frequently than my other friends. In that relationship, we regularly talk by phone whether the content is inconsequential or not. However, it is a compromise I willingly make because her friendship is important to me.

Before you decide whether or not a person embodies the qualities you desire in a friend, you must know what is negotiable. Don't willingly enter into a friendship with someone who has a quality that you will not tolerate. Be honest with yourself and others concerning your expectations. This will save you a lot of stress and conflict. Even if the person meets all of the above criteria, prayerfully consider whether or not you should enter into a friendship with her. Friends have the ability to impact your life significantly. They will either push you towards your destiny or derail you from it. Choose…them…wisely.

Lifeline: Don't willingly enter into a friendship with someone who has a quality that you will not tolerate.

CHAPTER 18

God, Our Ultimate Friend

And so it happened just as the Scriptures say: "Abraham believed God, and God counted him as righteous because of his faith." He was even called the friend of God. -James 2:23

No matter how healthy your friendships are, they will never compare to knowing and having God as your friend. Just as you communicate the intimate details of your life with your friends, you should also share your life with Him. To have a personal relationship with God, you must first acknowledge Him for who He is and accept His son Jesus. But, why?

The Bible tells us that all have fallen short of the standards of God. When you do so, it is called sin. That sin separates you from having a relationship with God and prevents you from living in eternity with Him. To bring you back into a loving relationship with Him, God sent His one and only son, Jesus, to die on the cross for you. After three days, Jesus rose from the dead and is now seated at the right hand of God praying and interceding on his children's behalf. To have a personal relationship with God, you must admit your sins and repent (turn in the opposite direction) of them. Then confess with your mouth that Jesus is Lord and believe in your hearts that God raised Him from the dead. The Bible promises that when you do so, you will be saved. If you want to know God and have a personal relationship with Him, pray the following prayer:

Lord God,

I come to you today acknowledging that I am a sinner who has fallen short of your standards. I recognize my need for you and ask that you forgive me of my sins. I confess that Jesus is Lord. I believe in my heart that you raised Him from the dead. I surrender my life to you. I receive your free gift of forgiveness, and I thank you for restoring me to a loving relationship with you. In Jesus' name, Amen.

If you have prayed this prayer, congratulations! Luke 15:7 tells us that the angels in Heaven are rejoicing over the decision you just made. You are now a member of the family of God which the Bible also refers to as the body of Christ. As a member of the body of Christ, you must connect yourself to other believers. Just as a hand cannot operate separately from the body, you cannot operate separately from the church. Immediately find a local church that teaches the Bible and begin studying the Bible for yourself. Get baptized which represents your new life in Christ. Then surround yourself with others who will encourage you in your faith.

Just as God called Abraham His friend, He now calls you His friend because of your new faith in Jesus Christ. Romans 5:11 tells us "So now we can rejoice in our wonderful new relationship with God because our Lord Jesus Christ has made us friends of God."

This new found friendship is both exciting and rewarding and comes with many benefits. Just like any good friend, God desires to see you succeed and will give you a helper that enables you to do so. That helper is called the Holy Spirit. The Holy Spirit will teach you and remind you of everything God has spoken and serve as a guide to you in your decisions (John 14:26, John 16:13). The Holy Spirit will also give you the power to do everything God leads you to do. It is a free gift given to every believer after putting faith in Jesus and getting baptized (Acts 2:38-39).

In addition to the Holy Spirit, a friendship with God offers the following and more:

- Peace (John 14:27)
- A hopeful future (Jeremiah 31:6)
- Constant companionship (Hebrews 13:5)
- Love (Jeremiah 31:3)
- Protection (2 Thessalonians 3:3)
- Confidence (Ephesians 3:12, 1 Peter 2:9-10)
- Freedom from condemnation (Colossians 1:22)
- Joy (Isaiah 61:3)

- A full supply of all your needs (Philippians 4:19)
- Restoration after suffering (1 Peter 5:10)
- Healing from a broken heart (Psalms 147:3)

As you begin to recognize the benefits of a friendship with God, you should also start thinking of ways to strengthen it. Get to know God more by reading His word and spending time with others who know Him as well. Make time in your schedule to share your heart with Him and listen as He shares His heart with you. Then be willing to make sacrifices and thank God for His sacrifice for you.

God loves you unconditionally and desires to be a part of every aspect of your life. He is not simply your Lord. He is the perfect, ultimate friend.

Scriptures on Friendship

No longer do I call you servants, for the servant does not know what his master is doing; but I have called you friends, for all that I have heard from my Father I have made known to you (John 15:15 ESV).

There is no greater love than to lay down one's life for one's friends (John 15:13).

Faithful are the wounds of a friend; profuse are the kisses of an enemy (Proverbs 27:6 ESV).

The righteous should choose his friends carefully, For the way of the wicked leads them astray (Proverbs 12:26 NKJV).

Do not be so deceived and misled! Evil companionships (communion, associations) corrupt and deprave good manners and morals and character (1 Corinthians 15:33 AMP).

A friend loves at all times, and is born, as is a brother, for adversity (Proverbs 17:17 AMP).

Wealth brings many new friends, but a poor man is deserted by his friend (Proverbs 19:4 ESV).

A man of many companions may come to ruin, but there is a friend who sticks closer than a brother (Proverbs 18:24 ESV).

An offended brother is harder to win back than a fortified city. Arguments separate friends like a gate locked with bars (Proverbs 18:19).

As iron sharpens iron, so a friend sharpens a friend (Proverbs 27:17).

Two people are better off than one, for they can help each other succeed. If one person falls, the other can reach out and help. But someone who falls alone is in real trouble. Likewise, two people lying close together can keep each other warm. But how can one be warm alone? A person standing alone can be attacked and defeated, but two can stand back-to-back and conquer. Three are even better, for a triple-braided cord is not easily broken (Ecclesiastes 4:9-12).

Qualities to look for & have

Calm temperance

Don't befriend angry people or associate with hot-tempered people, or you will learn to be like them and endanger your soul (Proverbs 22:24-25).

Wisdom

Walk with the wise and become wise; associate with fools and get in trouble (Proverbs 13:20).

Loving

A friend loves at all times, and a brother is born for adversity (Proverbs 17:17 ESV).

Keeps a confidence

A gossip goes around telling secrets, but those who are trustworthy can keep a confidence (Proverbs 11:13).

Gives good advice

The godly give good advice to their friends; the wicked lead them astray (Proverbs 12:26).

Oil and perfume make the heart glad, and the sweetness of a friend comes from his earnest counsel (Proverbs 27:6 ESV).

Loyalty

But Ruth said, "Do not urge me to leave you or to return from following you. For where you go I will go, and where you lodge I will lodge. Your people shall be my people, and your God my God. Where you die I will die, and there will I be buried. May the Lord do so to me and more also if anything but death parts me from you" (Ruth 1:16-17 ESV).

As soon as he had finished speaking to Saul, the soul of Jonathan was knit to the soul of David, and Jonathan loved him as his own soul. And Saul took him that day and would not let him return to his father's house. Then Jonathan made a covenant with David, because he loved him as his own soul. And Jonathan stripped himself of the robe that was on him and gave it to David, and his armor, and even his sword and his bow and his belt (1 Samuel 18:1-4 ESV).

Then Jonathan said to David, "Go in peace, because we have sworn both of us in the name of the Lord, saying, 'The Lord shall be between me and you, and between my offspring and your offspring, forever.'" And he rose and departed, and Jonathan went into the city (1 Samuel 20:12-13, 42 ESV).

Never abandon a friend – either yours or your father's. When disaster strikes, you won't have to ask your brother for assistance. It's better to go to a neighbor than to a brother who lives far away (Proverbs 27:10).

Faithful in adversity

And Saul spoke to Jonathan his son and to all his servants, that they should kill David. But Jonathan, Saul's son, delighted much in David. And Jonathan told David, "Saul my father seeks to kill you. Therefore be on your guard in the morning. Stay in a secret place and hide yourself. And I will go out and stand beside my father in the field where you are, and I will speak to my father about you. And if I learn anything I will tell you."

And Saul listened to the voice of Jonathan. Saul swore, "As the Lord lives, he shall not be put to death." And Jonathan called David, and Jonathan reported to him all these things. And Jonathan brought David to Saul, and he was in his presence as before (1 Samuel 19:1-3, 6-7 ESV).

And Jonathan said to David, "The Lord, the God of Israel, be witness! When I have sounded out my father, about this time tomorrow, or the third day, behold, if he is well disposed toward David, shall I not then send and disclose it to you? But should it please my father to do you harm, the Lord do so to Jonathan and more also if I do not disclose it to you and send you away, that you may go in safety. May the Lord be with you, as he has been with my father (1 Samuel 20:12-13 ESV).

Covers over offenses

Whoever covers an offense seeks love, but he who repeats a matter separates close friends (Proverbs 17:9 ESV).

Those seeking to do no harm

Who may worship in your sanctuary, LORD? Who may enter your presence on your holy hill? ....Those who refuse to gossip or harm their neighbors or speak evil of their friends (Psalms 15:1, 3).

Things to watch out for

Jealousy

A peaceful heart leads to a healthy body; jealousy is like cancer to the bones (Proverbs 14:30).

For anger slays the foolish man, And jealousy kills the simple (Job 5:2 NASB).

Wrath is fierce and anger is a flood, But who can stand before jealousy (Proverbs 27:4 NASB)?

Lack of Loyalty

Many will say they are loyal friends, but who can find one who is truly reliable (Proverbs 20:6)?

My companion stretched out his hand against his friends; he violated his covenant. His speech was smooth as butter, yet war was in his heart; his words were softer than oil, yet they were drawn swords. (Psalms 55:20-21 ESV).

Destruction/Betrayal

There are "friends" who destroy each other, but a real friend sticks closer than a brother (Proverbs 18:24).

With their words, the godless destroy their friends, but knowledge will rescue the righteous (Proverbs 11:9).

They confronted me in the day of my calamity, but the Lord was my support (Psalms 18:18 ESV).

Even my close friend in whom I trusted, who ate my bread, has lifted his heel against me (Psalms 41:9 ESV).

For it is not an enemy who taunts me—then I could bear it; it is not an adversary who deals insolently with me—then I could hide from him. But it is you, a man, my equal, my companion, my familiar friend (Psalm 55:12 ESV).

Selfishness

Unfriendly people care only about themselves; they lash out at common sense (Proverbs 18:1).

Gossip/speaking evil

Who may worship in your sanctuary, LORD? Who may enter your presence on your holy hill?...Those who refuse to gossip or harm their neighbors or speak evil of their friends (Psalms 15: 1,3).

Endnotes

Chapter 1

1. Strong's Greek: 5384. φίλος (philos) -- beloved, dear, friendly. (n.d.). Retrieved June 20, 2015, from http://biblehub.com/greek/5384.htm

Chapter 2

2. Strong, James (1990). Loveth. In *The New Strong's Exhaustive concordance of the Bible* (pp. 9) Nashville, TN: THOMAS NELSON.

Chapter 4

3. UCLA Researchers Identify Key Biobehavioral Pattern Used by Women to Manage Stress. (n.d.). Retrieved February 10, 2015, from http://newsroom.ucla.edu/releases/UCLA-Researchers-Identify-Key-Biobehavioral-1478

4. Why dishing does you good: U-M study | University of Michigan News. (n.d.). Retrieved February 10, 2015, from

http://ns.umich.edu/new/releases/7181-why-dishing-does-you-good-u-m-study

5. Good Friendships. Great Health. - Texas Conference for Women. (2010). Retrieved February 10, 2015, from https://www.txconferenceforwomen.org/good-friendships-great-health/

6. Umberson, D., & Montez, J. K. (2010). Social Relationships and Health: A Flashpoint for Health Policy. Retrieved February 10, 2015, from http://www.ncbi.nlm.nih.gov/pmc/articles/PMC3 150158/

Chapter 5

7. Davis, S. Z. (2009). The friends we keep: A woman's quest for the soul of friendship. Colorado Springs, CO: WaterBrook Press.

8. Barash, S. S. (2009). Toxic friends: The antidote for women stuck in complicated friendships. New York, NY: St. Martin's Press.

Chapter 6

9. Strong's Greek: 1259. διαλλάσσω (diallassó) -- change, exchange. (n.d.). Retrieved June 12, 2016,

from http://biblehub.com/greek/1259.htm

10. (n.d.). Retrieved November 12, 2015, from http://www.merriam-webster.com/dictionary/reconcile

11. Ahitophel. (n.d.). Retrieved October 10, 2015, from https://en.wikipedia.org/wiki/Ahitophel

Chapter 7

12. Barash, S. S. (2009). Toxic friends: The antidote for women stuck in complicated friendships. New York, NY: St. Martin's Press.

13. Goldsmith-Thomas, Elaine, Schindler, Deborah, Sherak, William & Shuman, Jason (Producers), Huran, Nick (Director). (2004). *Little Black Book* [Motion Picture]. United States: Revolution Studios.

Chapter 8

14. Strong's Greek: 863. ἀφίημι (aphiémi) -- to send away, leave alone, permit. (n.d.). Retrieved January 12, 2016, from http://biblehub.com/greek/863.htm

67891297R00070

Made in the USA
Charleston, SC
27 February 2017